Spider Boy!

by Stan Cullimore

Characters: **Narrator**
Sam – the hero.
Dan – his little brother.
Big Billy – the school bully.
Mr Watt – a man who owns a pet shop.

Scene 1: *On the High Street, after school one day.*

Narrator Sam was a quiet boy - this meant two things. One, he did not have very many friends...

Big Billy Hello, Spider Boy!

Narrator And two, Big Billy picked on him all the time...

Sam I've told you before, Billy. My name is not Spider Boy, it's Sam.

Narrator Big Billy was the school bully.

Big Billy What did you say, Spider Boy?

Sam I said, my name is not Spider Boy, it's Sam.

Narrator Big Billy looked around as if he could not believe his ears.

Big Billy Who said that?

 2

Narrator   Sam sighed. He knew what was coming next.
Big Billy had done this many times before…

Sam   I did.

Big Billy   Wow! I didn't know that spiders could talk!

Sam   They can't.

Big Billy   But you just did!

Sam   That's because I'm *not* a spider.

Big Billy   Aren't you?

Sam   No.

Big Billy   Well you could have fooled me. You look just
like one.

Sam   No, I don't.

Big Billy   Yes, you do. You've got long skinny legs just like
a spider's!

Narrator   Sam sighed.

Sam   I don't think so.

Narrator   The trouble was that Sam *did* have very long,
thin legs - and he knew it…

 3

Big Billy And you walk all funny!

Sam No, I don't.

Big Billy Yes, you do. You walk just like a spider.

Narrator By now the two boys were standing outside a pet shop. Sam stopped.

Big Billy Look, a pet shop!

Sam I know, I'm going in to have a look around.

Big Billy I don't think that's a very good idea, Spider Boy.

Sam Why not?

Big Billy Well, they might think that you have escaped from out of one of the cages.

Sam I don't think so.

Big Billy One of the spider cages!

Narrator Sam opened the door of the shop.

Big Billy They might not let you back out of the shop again!

 4

Sam   Mr Watt is a friend of mine. I don't think he'll get me mixed up with one of his spiders.

Narrator Mr Watt was the man who owned the pet shop.

Big Billy Don't count on it, Spider Boy!

Narrator Big Billy smiled.

Big Billy I know why you're going into that shop.You're looking for some flies aren't you?

Sam   Why would I look for flies?

Big Billy Because that's what spiders eat, isn't it?

Narrator With that Big Billy walked off down the street, laughing to himself.

Scene 2: *A few seconds later, inside the shop.*

Narrator   There was a small man standing behind the counter in the shop. It was Mr Watt.

Mr Watt   Hello, Sam. How are you today?

Sam   Not very well.

Mr Watt   Why not?

Sam   It's Big Billy. He's the school bully. He's always picking on me and calling me names.

Mr Watt   What sort of names?

Sam   He calls me Spider Boy.

Mr Watt   Why?

Sam   Because he thinks I look like a spider.

Mr Watt   I see.

Narrator   Mr Watt looked thoughtful.

Mr Watt   The trouble is, Sam… if you don't stand up to bullies they often just get worse and worse.

 6

Sam	I know. But what can I do about it? Billy *is* very big and he's much stronger than me. I can't really stand up to him, can I?
Mr Watt	Perhaps not, we'll have to see.
Narrator	Mr Watt bent down and picked up a small spider cage that was under the counter.
Mr Watt	This will cheer you up.
Sam	What is it?
Mr Watt	A very, very rare spider. It's from Tibet and it has blue knees. It's called a 'Dream Spider'.
Narrator	Mr Watt gave the cage to Sam.
Mr Watt	Can you look after it for me?
Sam	Can I? I'd love to.
Mr Watt	Good. There is one thing... I want you to promise that you will bring it straight back to me if it bites you.
Sam	OK. I promise.
Narrator	With that, Sam picked up the spider cage and went home.

Scene 3: *The next morning, at Sam's house. Breakfast time.*

Sam   Hey, Dan!

Narrator   Dan was Sam's younger brother.

Dan   What?

Sam   You know that spider I told you about?

Dan   The one you got from Mr Watt?

Sam   Yes.

Dan   The one with funny knees.

Sam   The one with *blue* knees - that's right.

Dan   What about it?

Sam   I took it out of its cage last night.

Narrator   Dan took a bite out of his piece of toast.

Dan   Has it really got blue knees?

Sam   Yes.

Dan   Why?

Sam   Why has it got blue knees?

Dan   Yes.

Sam   I don't know. Mr Watt says that all 'Dream
Spiders' have them.

Dan   Doesn't sound right to me. I think spiders
should have black knees - or brown.

Sam   Dan?

Dan   What?

Sam   Will you shut up and listen for a minute?

Narrator Dan nodded. Then he took another bite of toast.

Sam   When I took the spider out of its cage last
night, it bit me.

Dan   Why?

Sam   I don't know. Anyway, I'm going to take it back
to Mr Watt after school today.

Dan   Is that all you wanted to say?

Narrator Sam shook his head.

Sam   No, there's more. I had a really strange dream last night.

Dan   What about?

Sam   I dreamt that I was a spider.

Dan   What colour were your knees?

Sam   Pardon?

Dan   What colour were your knees? Were they black - or brown?

Narrator Sam frowned.

Sam   Neither. They were blue.

Dan   That doesn't sound right to me. Spiders should always have black knees - or brown.

Narrator Sam looked thoughtful.

Sam   So I must have been a 'Dream Spider.'

Dan   Did anything happen in this dream of yours?

Sam   Yes.

Dan   What?

10

Sam   I made a web.

Dan   Is that all?

Sam   No. I trapped some flies.

Dan   Did you eat any of them?

Sam   Yes, I did.

Dan   I bet they didn't taste very nice!

Sam   Actually, they weren't that bad. I quite liked them.

Dan   Now that really is strange!

Narrator Dan stood up.

Dan   Anyway, I'm off to school. Are you coming?

Sam   In a minute. I've got to go and clean my teeth first.

Dan   OK. I'll see you there. Catch you later.

Sam   OK.

Scene 4: *A few seconds later, in the bathroom.*

Narrator   Sam went into the bathroom and picked up his toothbrush. He began to clean his teeth.

Sam   Hang on.

Narrator   He took his toothbrush out of his mouth.

Sam   What's that?

Narrator   There was something stuck between his teeth.

Sam   It must be a piece of toast, I suppose.

Narrator   Sam looked in the mirror and carefully pulled out the thing that was stuck between his teeth.

Sam   That's strange.

Narrator   He frowned at it.

Sam   It doesn't look anything like toast!

Narrator   He frowned at it again.

Sam   It looks more like… a fly's wing!

Narrator   He looked at himself in the mirror.

Sam   How on earth did I get a fly's wing stuck
             between my teeth?

Narrator He slowly put his toothbrush back in its cup and
             went downstairs. He looked very thoughtful...

 13

Scene 5: *After school that same day. In the pet shop.*

Narrator Mr Watt was standing behind the counter. He was watching the people go past outside the window.

Mr Watt It's very busy out there today! There are lots of people on the High Street.

Narrator He smiled as the door opened…

Mr Watt Hello, Sam. How are you today?

Sam Well…

Narrator Sam thought for a minute.

Sam I'm not sure really.

Mr Watt Why not?

Sam It's been a very strange day.

Mr Watt What do you mean?

Narrator Sam reached into his bag and pulled out the 'Dream Spider' cage.

Sam Well, for a start. I've got to give this back to you…

Mr Watt Why?

 14

Sam   I took the 'Dream Spider' out of its cage last night…

Mr Watt   Something happened did it?

Sam   Yes.

Mr Watt   What?

Sam   It bit me!

Mr Watt   No!

Sam   Yes!

Mr Watt   You lucky thing!

Sam   Lucky?

Mr Watt   Yes.

Sam   Why am I lucky?

Mr Watt   Because the 'Dream Spider' has never bitten me! I've taken it out of its cage lots of times.

Narrator   Sam shook his head. He couldn't understand why Mr Watt seemed so excited.

Sam   Anyway, as I said, it bit me…

 15

Mr Watt   Did you have any funny dreams last night?

Sam   Yes, I did.

Mr Watt   What did you dream about?

Sam   I dreamt that I was a spider - a 'Dream Spider.'

Mr Watt   How do you know that you were a 'Dream Spider?'

Sam   Because I had blue knees!

Mr Watt   You really are lucky!

Sam   I don't think so!

Mr Watt   Why not?

Sam   I told you. It bit me.

Mr Watt   You lucky old thing!

Sam   ...and then this morning Big Billy pushed me over in the playground!

Mr Watt   He's the school bully, isn't he?

Sam   Yes.

Mr Watt   The one who calls you names?

Sam That's right. Anyway, after he pushed me over, he punched me.

Narrator Mr Watt nodded his head.

Mr Watt I thought that he would get worse. Bullies always do!

Sam He's a real pain.

Mr Watt Tell me, Sam - how did you feel when Big Billy pushed you?

Sam What?

Mr Watt I mean - did you like it?

Sam No, of course I didn't!

Mr Watt So how did it make you feel?

Narrator Mr Watt looked at Sam thoughtfully.

Sam Angry! It made me feel angry.

Narrator Sam clenched his fists.

Mr Watt That's good!

Sam I wanted to hit Big Billy and stop him from being horrid to me.

Mr Watt	So why didn't you do that, Sam?
Sam	Because he would have punched me again. Only harder!
Mr Watt	Do you know what I think, Sam?
Sam	What?
Mr Watt	I think that the next time Big Billy tries to bully you, you should *use* your anger.
Sam	What do you mean?
Mr Watt	I mean that you should *use* your anger to show Big Billy how it feels to be bullied.
Sam	But how can I do that? He's much bigger than me!
Mr Watt	It doesn't matter! Just imagine that you are a giant spider and that Big Billy is a little fly trapped in your web…
Sam	What good will that do? He'll just laugh at me.
Narrator	Mr Watt smiled.
Mr Watt	I don't think he will, you know.
Sam	Why not?

Mr Watt   Do you remember your dream, Sam?

Sam   Yes, I do. What about it?

Mr Watt   I think it might be trying to tell you something.

Sam   Like what?

Mr Watt   I think it might be trying to tell you that *you* are a 'Dream Spider' now.

Narrator   Sam laughed.

Sam   No way! It was only a dream.

Mr Watt   Was it?

Narrator   Sam was just about to answer, when he remembered what he had found when he cleaned his teeth that morning...

Sam   That's a point...

Mr Watt   What is?

Sam   Where did the fly's wing come from?

Mr Watt   What?

Sam   Nothing! I'd better be off, Mr Watt - I'll be late for tea. Goodbye.

Scene 6: *The next morning. On the way to school.*

Narrator The next morning Sam and Dan walked to school.

Sam You know what, Dan?

Dan What?

Sam I had another dream last night.

Dan What about?

Sam Being a spider.

Dan Did you have blue knees again?

Sam Yes.

Dan I still think that's strange!

Narrator By now the two boys were walking along the High Street.

Sam It really felt like I *was* a spider, you know.

Big Billy Hello, Spider Boy!

Sam Go away, Billy.

Big Billy Hey. This must be your little brother.

Narrator   Billy got hold of Dan's school bag and threw it on the ground.

Big Billy   Look! He's dropped his bag. What a pity!

Sam   Leave him alone, Billy!

Big Billy   Shut up, Spider Boy!

Sam   Dan, off you go. You'll be late. I'll see you in school.

Narrator   Dan picked up his bag and ran off.

Big Billy   Right, give it to me.

Sam   What?

Big Billy   Your dinner money - or else I'll beat you up!

Sam   My dinner money?

Big Billy   That's right!

Sam   Mr Watt was right. Bullies do always get worse!

Big Billy   What?

Narrator   Sam suddenly remembered what else Mr Watt had said. He had to *use* his anger.

21

Sam   Here goes.

Narrator   Sam closed his eyes - and was back in his dream once more.

Sam   Very nice!

Narrator   He was a giant spider. Billy was a fly - a nice juicy little fly. The perfect breakfast...

Sam   Come here, little fly!

Narrator   Sam began to walk forwards. He licked his lips.

Sam   Very tasty!

Narrator   Suddenly Sam opened his eyes. He could hear someone screaming. He looked around.

Sam   What's wrong, Billy?

Narrator   But Billy didn't answer. He had run away - in tears!

Sam   What happened?

Narrator   Just then, Mr. Watt appeared.

Mr Watt   Hello, Sam. What's going on?

Sam   I'm not really sure!

Mr Watt   Why not?

Narrator   Sam laughed.

Sam   You'll never believe me, even if I tell you.

Mr Watt   Try me!

Sam   Do you remember what you said? About *using* my anger next time Big Billy tried to bully me?

Mr Watt   Yes, I do.

Sam   Well that's what I just did.

Mr Watt   Really?

Sam   Yes. I imagined that I was a giant spider and that Billy was a little fly trapped in my web.

Mr Watt   What happened?

Sam   He ran away. It was amazing!

Mr Watt   Was it?

Sam   Yes. For one minute, I really *did* feel like a spider. A real spider!

Narrator Mr Watt looked down.

Mr Watt I'm not surprised. Look at your knees!

Narrator Sam looked down.

Sam But... how did that happen?

Narrator His knees had changed colour. They were blue...

Mr Watt I don't think you will have any more trouble from Big Billy, Sam. I told you the dream was trying to tell you something.

Sam But what?

Mr Watt You *really* are a Spider Boy now! A 'Dream Spider' boy!

THE END